W9-ABV-280

Boise State University Western Writers Series Number 19

Robinson Jeffers

By Robert J. Brophy

California State University

Long Beach

Editors: Wayne Chatterton
James H. Maguire

Business Manager:
James Hadden

Cover Design and Illustration
by Arny Skov, Copyright 1975

Boise State University, Boise, Idaho

Printed in the United States of America by
The Caxton Printers, Ltd.
Caldwell, Idaho

Robinson Jeffers

CORRIGENDA

The following errors were inadvertently introduced into the manuscript during the editing process and are not the fault of the author.

Page 5:   Robinson and Una were married in 1913, not 1914.

Page 6:   Robinson's birth year was 1887, not 1885.

Page 7:   Robinson Jeffers was not an only child but had a brother, seven years his junior, born in 1894, Hamilton Jeffers, who was to become a noted astronomer at Lick Observatory.

Page 9:   The love affair was clandestine and only became a scandal at the time of Una Kuster's divorce and her marriage to Jeffers.

Robinson Jeffers

By temperament an isolate and contemplative, Robinson Jeffers has been repeatdly characterized as the hermit, guardian, and interpreter of the westernmost coast. In his long literary career from *Flagons and Apples* in 1912 to *The Beginning and The End* in 1963, he wrote almost exclusively in one genre, poetry. Poetry was for him a searing vehicle of truth. "I can tell lies in prose" was his sentiment.

From his pen came over thirty-five narratives from two to 175 pages long, and an outpouring of more than 300 lyrics. His story-poems can be divided into narrative, semi-dramatic, and dramatic pieces. His lyrics are either short responses, characteristically grouped around the narrative of each volume as variations on its theme, or two- to five-page philosophical meditations upon man's choices, upon man's delusions, and upon man's chances for peace. All his poetry has the same foundation —the rock shore of the final sea, the rugged headland coast overlooking the Pacific.

His early life was characterized by mobility and by what appears to have been family instability. But shortly after he had married Una in 1914, Jeffers settled into his "inevitable place," a lonely knoll on the Carmel peninsula in California. There, stone by stone, he built Tor House and Hawk Tower. To the west was the immense water stretching toward Asia, and to the south was the magnificent landscape which is the Carmel-Sur coastline. For the remaining fifty-eight years of his life he never left this vantage point on the "edge of the world" except for a few Una-inspired excursions to Ireland and some shorter trips to Taos and the East coast. Born an Easterner, educated primarily in Europe, he became a Westerner as few others have. His coast, "The Continent's End," became the medium of his interpretation of the whole of life, history, and art.

He was born in Pennsylvania on January 10, 1885, and was baptized John Robinson. His parents were Annie Tuttle and William Hamilton Jeffers. In speaking of his origins and formative years, he once told a correspondent that as a child he was taken to Europe a few times, but that the trips made little impression upon his immature mind. His intellectual development, however, was rigorous and sophisticated.

> When I was nine years old my father began to slap latin into me, literally, with his hands; and when I was eleven he put me in a boarding school in Switzerland— a new one every year for four years—Vevey, Lausanne, Geneva, Zurich. Then he brought me home and put me in college as a sophomore. I graduated accordingly at eighteen, not that I was intelligent but by sporting my languages and avoiding mathematics. Then, I took postgraduate studies in English and European literatures, even a little forestry, finally three years in medical school—not knowing what else to do; and then drifted into mere drunken idleness. (*Selected Letters,* No. 377).

His father was a strict disciplinarian. A professor of Old Testament Literature and Exegesis at Western Theological Seminary in Allegheny, a suburb of Pittsburgh, Dr. Jeffers had a distinguished teaching career. The death of a wife and child and almost fifty years of life were already behind him when he met and married Annie Tuttle, who played the organ in a little church where he served as visiting pastor. She was about twenty-five years younger than her new husband and was dra-

6

matically his opposite in temperament. Instead of taking her on a honeymoon, he moved her into a forbidding seminary housing unit.

Freudian analysts make much of this pattern—a young girl, long orphaned, never having known a father, falls in love with a man almost twice her age, a father figure with a set, secure life-pattern. She then has a son upon whom she can shed the emotional fervor forbidden by the father-husband relationship. The father recognizes the child as his rival, and the child becomes the center of reactions and manipulations. But whatever the most accurate analysis of their marriage might be, the fact is that Dr. W. Hamilton Jeffers and Annie Tuttle produced their only offspring about a year and a half after the union.

Robinson's first years were filled with exercises, both mental ones and stoically physical ones, which were evidently meant to shape him to his father's image. This image required of the little boy discipline, restraint, memorization, gradual isolation from playmates, stilted language, and ubiquitous seriousness. In 1898 Jeffers began the European sojourn which was characterized by systematic uprooting and re-enforcement of his Spartan temperament. In 1902 he returned to the United States to begin college—first at the University of Western Pennsylvania and then at Occidental College, a Presbyterian school in Los Angeles, where his father had moved for his health. Robinson graduated in a class of eleven in 1905 and entered graduate school at the University of Southern California.

By this time he seems to have begun a definitive break from the authoritarian, closed world of his father's creation. He moved away from home to a beach setting, where he began drinking and pursuing a series of love affairs. At USC he met his future wife, Una, in a German class on Faust. In April 1906 he began attending the University of Zurich (accompanying his parents once more), where he specialized in Philosophy, Old English, Dante, and Spanish literature. By 1907

7

he was back in Los Angeles at the University of Southern California Medical School. He soon ranked highest in his class, became special assistant to his physiology professor, and taught physiology at the USC Dental College. He also took part in fraternity activities and in a sports program that included swimming, track, and wrestling. During this time his involvement with Una continued. In 1910 his family moved to Seattle so that he could begin studying forestry at the University of Washington. Here he returned to finish his studies in 1913, just before he married Una.

Jeffers' formal education, though impressive in its challenge and intensity, may seem eclectic and haphazard. It might appear to be the result of rudderless family wandering rather than of a chartered career. But in retrospect everything somehow fits beautifully into place. His understanding of languages enabled him to leap geographic barriers, to range through centuries and cultures. It provided him with a precise knowledge of words. Religious education evidently instilled in him an intense questioning, an expectation of God, and a rich biblical fund of language, archetype, myth, and symbol. Science gave him an astronomic imagination, a sense of apocalyptic immanence, and the recognition of correspondences from atom to solar system to galaxy. Medicine urged upon him an iconoclastic view of man's life-pretensions, along with a clinical knowledge of pain, death, and corruption of the flesh. Classical literature opened to him a knowledge of the Greek dramatists, whose myth patterns lent themselves so readily to ritual drama, which became his own genre. Old English literature gave him the alternative to the metered verse of his time. Philosophy opened doors to Heraclitus and Lucretius, but primarily to Nietzsche and Schopenhauer—each of whom left his mark on the poet's thinking. The study of forestry was a unique contribution to his life and art. His knowledge of trees and flowers fills his poetry, and his therapeutic planting of thousands of eucalyptus and cypress at Tor House later gave him shelter from encroaching civilization. However, formal education surely was only a small part of the rich cultural background which Jeffers brought to his work. Throughout his life he read voluminously, as his correspondence will attest. Nevertheless the academic preparation certainly set the directions.

Jeffers was to identify the two great influences upon his life and poetry as the Carmel landscape and his wife, Una. The landscape became both his medium and his message, the setting and the protagonist. Even Jeffers' visage took on the craggy, rough, weathered, inscrutable character of this landscape. Una Jeffers was his life. His career is inconceivable without her. She was an emigrant from Michigan, and during her years at the University of California at Berkeley, she had married a young barrister named Edward Kuster. They had settled in Los Angeles so that he could launch his career as a lawyer, and she lived a rich cultural and social life while she finished work on her degree at the University of Southern California. But in a German class at the University she met Robinson Jeffers, and for seven years their love affair was something of a scandal in the community, rating headlines in two local papers when she divorced her husband and married Jeffers in Tacoma in August of 1913. Of her influence upon his life and writings he tells us:

> My nature is cold and undiscriminating; she excited and focused it, gave it eyes and nerves and sympathies. She never saw any of my poems until they were finished and typed, yet by her presence and conversation she has co-authored every one of them. Sometimes I think there must be some value in them, if only for that reason. She is more like a woman in a Scotch ballad, passionate, untamed and rather heroic—or like a falcon—than like any ordinary person. (*Selected Poetry,* xv)

9

Jeffers' overview of life, his philosophy, his system of values, seems to have been clear-cut from the beginning of his mature period (*Tamar,* 1924). Few poets have developed such a consistent and thorough-going world view. For Jeffers the answers are all there. One need only look without blinding bias. For him the cosmos moved in cyclic evolution, in the *whole* (oscillating universe hypothesis) and in all its *parts.* "Being" implies change, violence, and pain; yet it is transcendentally beautiful and divine. There is only matter and energy; no spirit or soul, no immortal realms. God is the "Beauty of things," a Self-Torturer who endures for the constant self-discovery ("At the Birth of an age"). Men are temporary phenomena, a problem in the universe because of their megalomanic, incestuous self-regard. But they are also, for their "moment" in being, a sense organ of God ("The Beginning and the End").

Consciousness is a universal quality in the cosmos, but man's mind, grotesquely self-magnifying and perverse, is not preeminent and will pass ("Credo"). Beauty remains even after the loss of man's ability to perceive it. Death ends individual existence, but the body is reassimilated into soil and air ("Hungerfield"). The world as a whole is determined. Civilizations inexorably rise and fall. Man's actions *en masse* are fated, but individuals can choose to step out, i.e., not to take part in corruption ("Shine Perishing Republic"). God is nothing like man, for God is savage, indifferent, wild ("Hurt Hawks"), encompassing both good and evil ("Contemplation of the Sword"). All things are sacred, in harmony. Evil is a part of the mosaic of Beauty, marking the close of the cycle.

Virtue lies principally in detachment, indifference, and stoicism—in turning outward and worshipping God. Wisdom means perspective, "uncentering" from man (inhumanism), seeing things from God's cosmic perspective ("Signpost"). Peace is stoic balance, which counters the innate biases for immortality, invulnerability, stability, immunity from pain and sickness. The idealistic should fear most the subtle savior syndrome which deludes man into believing that he can change the world. The aim is lofty, but it is only a delusion ("Rearmament"). Love is incestuous unless it is a love of the God perceived by Jeffers. Piety lies in reverence for Beauty (natural and cosmic), which is divine and which demands worship. The poet is reconciler—putting sin, guilt, corruption, pain, and all other confounding things into a context. The "good man" is not a leader, a rebel, or a savior. He is a mystic.

Jeffers' art was an intimate part of his life. It was a consequence of his philosophy, a religious vocation. The theme of every poem was the incredible, dynamic, divine beauty of the cosmos and the mutability of man. Every poem can be returned to this idea. If a single word can sum up Jeffers' philosophic and esthetic vision, it is the word "cycle." Cycle was the truth of the stars, the life of the planet, the fate of man, insect, and flower. "Cycle" moves through birth, growth, fulness, decay, death. In ritual terms "cycle" becomes translated into sacrifice (fragmentation) and sacrament (reintegration). "Cycle" is the elemental truth underlying all being.

Jeffers comprehends all reality in a *formula* implicit in "Apology for Bad Dreams": Being=Dynamism-Change=Pain-Tragedy=Beauty=God. Being is by nature dynamic, constantly changing. All things resist change because change means that things must give up a part or all of their essence. Change comes mostly through violence, whether the violence is dramatic or subtle. Violence makes sentient beings respond with pain. Pain and violence are therefore the essence of the terrible beauty which is tragedy, which is God. Though modern man flees the metaphysical implications of the cycle, primitive man accepted and celebrated them. Each year the cycle god (Dionysus, Osiris, Tammuz, Attis) had to suffer the consequences of re-entry into life, since he was born in order to die. Decline and death were not blameworthy but inevitable.

11

Subsidiary themes, of course, abound in Jeffers' poetry, but they all reflect the cycle—human mutability, reconciliation to evil, confrontation of pain, indifference achieved by cosmic perspective, the nature of wisdom, stoicism, acceptance of God, beauty of death and annihilation, inevitability of processes, delusion of effectiveness, presumptuousness of man's self-importance, the nature of the poet's art, the centrality of tragedy, the omnipresence and the beauty of violence. These are all patterns in the search for truth, authentic piety, true peace.

Jeffers once called his over-riding philosophy "inhumanism." In the preface to *The Double Axe* he describes "inhumanism":

> a shifting of emphasis and significance from man to not-man; the rejection of human solipsism and recognition of the transhuman magnificence. It seems time that our race began to think as an adult does, rather than like an egocentric baby or insane person. This manner of thought and feeling is neither misanthropic nor pessimist, though two or three people have said so and may again. It involves no falsehoods, and is a means of maintaining sanity in slippery times; it has objective truth and human value. It offers a reasonable detachment as a rule of conduct, instead of love, hate and envy. It neutralizes fanaticism and wild hopes; but it provides magnificence for the religious instinct, and satisfies our need to admire greatness and rejoice in beauty.

But about his own aesthetics Jeffers wrote no manifestos. Most of what he has to say he says in passing. In his foreword to *Selected Poetry* (1938) he declares his intention to reclaim the power and reality which poetry has surrendered to prose, poetry here being especially the Symbolist drift toward the slight, fantastic, abstract, and unreal. He meant to write so that he would be understood by the reader 2000 years away. Poetry was to be

about permanent things, the eternally recurring ("Point Joe").
He promised not to pretend anything, especially not optimism
or pessimism. He vowed to eschew the popular, the accepted,
the fashionable. He would not believe easily, but he would
speak what he believed, whatever the consequences.

On one level at least, many of his poems seem to be reflections
upon the poetic vocation. "Apology for Bad Dreams" tells us
that he writes poetry for his own salvation and for the salvation of his readers. He writes to reconcile man's perversity with
the beauty of things, as in the image of a woman beating a
horse, coupled with the image of the Sur coast at sundown.
Landscape demands tragedy, and beauty demands its proportion
of pain. As in horror stories like "Tamar," the poet writes his
bad dreams in order to avoid the terror that blinds and turns
one inward. He does this for several reasons. Perhaps he hopes
to educate himself by learning violence and cycle in order to
accept them. Perhaps as a form of therapy he wants to write
out his violences lest he act them out instead. Or perhaps he
seeks to participate in ritual by living on a level of discovery
that parallels that of God.

The purpose of art is discovery. The poet "brays" humanity
in a crucible to bring out the essence of art, to discover the
workings of reality. In all things there is no reason, only cycle
and pain and beauty to be savored. The short narrative "An
Artist" tells the same story as "Apology." The artist of the
poem works with grotesques which have pain-filled eyes because
only these can see God and only these are worthy of the world's
earnest beauty.

Jeffers' sense of art is always a religious one, a ministerial
one. In "Night" his poem is a "prayer" trying to encompass
God, a prayer that stumbles and stutters before the overwhelm-
ing and the ineffable. Jeffers' "Crumbs or the Loaf" adapts
Jesus' explanation which follows the parable of the Sower
(Matthew 13). Here Jeffers says that he too speaks through

both parable, which is the crumbs, and apodictic sayings, which is the loaf. Parable, however, is the more subtle and therefore the more palatable. Jeffers sees his narratives as parabolic statements and his lyrics as head-on confrontations with truth, as indicated by these injunctions: take up your cross . . . hate father, mother, and your own life . . . unless the grain of wheat fall into the ground and die. . . .

The invocation in "Tamar" (V) calls upon the God of Beauty to enter into Jeffers "puppets" and speak through them—because God typically chooses grotesques, makes music through "crooked bugles," makes signs of sins, and chooses the lame for angels. The invocation to "The Woman at Point Sur" is in the same mode. The parable characters, grotesque though they may be, are there to praise God, as Jeffers indicates by the line "I made glass puppets to speak of him, they splintered in my hand." These characters have gone mad, but they still "stammer the tragedy." In the "Prelude" to the same poem, Jeffers says, "But why should I make fables again? There are many / Tellers of tales to delight women and the people. / I have no vocation [for entertainment]." "I said, 'Humanity is the start of the race, the gate to break away from, the coal to kindle, the blind mask crying to be slit with eye holes' "—that is, in order to see, through parables. In a lyric interlude to "Roan Stallion," Jeffers tells us that tragedy—as he sees it and writes it—is to break man out of himself, to act as a shock treatment, shattering the patterns of schizophrenia and paranoia, and opening the mind to new patterns which can encompass God and the cosmic whole.

In 1948 Jeffers was prevailed upon to write his thoughts about poetry for the New York *Times* magazine section. His response was that poetry is not bound by time and circumstance, nor does it need a large audience. The truly great poet does not imitate nor join a school. He turns from self-consciousness, naive learnedness, undergraduate irony, and labored obscurity.

He is natural and direct, has something ever new and important to say, and wants to say it clearly in the spirit of his time and of all time. His poetry is pointed at the future and will be understood for a thousand years because it illuminates essential things. Jeffers' only other substantial prose statement on art, a lecture which he delivered at the Library of Congress and which was published as *Themes in My Poems* (1956), is founded upon his previous vocational affirmations, and it illustrates his themes. From these themes he singles out Death, War, Culture-Cycles, Pantheism, Beauty, The Self-Torturing God, Landscape as actor and revelation, Hawk as spirit of the place, and Poetry itself as discovery and God-like creation.

Jeffers' poetic form has at times baffled critics. He early renounced rhyme and meter. Instead, his lines are usually measured by accentual beat, as in biblical poetry and Old English epic. The number of beats varies with the intent of the poem, but especially in the narratives the beat is regular and quite predictable. In his short poems he sometimes surprises the reader with a sonnet perfectly turned ("To His Father," "Love the Wild Swan"). But more often the poems seek their own form through some sort of dialectic, such as the monologues of "Soliloquy" and "Self-Criticism in February." The lyrics make use of occasional alliteration ("Continent's End") and of long and short lines, the longer usually being reserved for the more philosophic and meditative poems.

Jeffers' imagery carries much of his poetic message. Image patterns in "Tamar," for instance, anticipate the denouement long before the story action ever reaches the crisis. In fact, first-page images frequently mimic the catastrophe and the final lines. As one can predict, his images are heavily cyclic: wave, tide, season, day and night, equinox and solstice, constellation change, moon phase, breath, heartbeat, pulse, music, and dance. Images are often cosmogonic, having to do with sacrifice and sacrament as the recurring ritual of creation and renewal. Jef-

15

fers sometimes evokes the cosmic horse ("Roan Stallion"), the cosmic giant ("At the Birth of an Age"), and the cosmic eagle ("Cawdor"). In ancient cosmogonies the animal, god, or goddess was sacrificed, whereupon the body became the land, the blood became the seas and rivers, the hair or mane became the vegetation. Such a cosmogony is a paradigm of the multi-level fragmentation, the reintegration, the beauty, and the divinity of reality itself. The images are always recognizable as part of Jeffers' coastal scene. At the same time they operate as the archetypes of rock, sea, star, tree, night, fountain, or center; as the rituals of blood, cross, sunset, or dance; as the myths of wound, flower, or surrogate animal; and as the apocalypse represented by fire, quake, storm, or deluge.

Jeffers calls his narrative poems "tragedies." The poet's notion of "tragedy" is even more ancient and more basic than the form used by the classical Greek tragedians. Indeed, cultural anthropologists tell us that the "primitive" tragedies which celebrated the cyclic life-death pattern of the year-god were the *origin* of Greek drama. The year-spirit, or Dionysian god, was dressed up as hero—Hippolytus, Jason, Agamemnon, Oedipus—and was destroyed at the turn of the year to restore balance to the world.

Jeffers adapts old myths, biblical and classical, Mediterranean and Norse, in order to bespeak the death-resurrection pattern which is central to the primitive religions that celebrated the yearly cycle as the life span of the fertility god. The ancients believed that the god appeared and was reunited with the goddess (Spring), matured and was tested (Summer), rejected his goddess-consort and fertility principle (Fall), and was torn by animals, by an enemy, or by some agent of the goddess, and then died and was buried (Winter), to be lamented until his Spring resurrection and epiphany. Jeffers' heroes limp with the year-God's limp and are hanged, torn, thigh-wounded, or emasculated as were Odin, Hippolytus, Dionysus, Attis, and Orion. In

16

"My Loved Subject" Jeffers tells us that the protagonists of his poems are not really men but in fact the landscape, which in turn interprets the cosmos. His human characters enact the divine ritual of the universe in man's peculiar terms and are meant to counter man's peculiar biases or astigmatisms.

Jeffers' stories are rituals of mutability. The ritual itself is impersonal, inexorable, autonomic, repetitious, undergirding all things at all levels. The protagonists thereby are not psychological studies in themselves. As Jeffers says, they are barely believable puppets which act out the Punch and Judy show that is reality. They teach variously indifference to power, freedom from guilt, access to god, conquest of fears, and other lessons which are implicit in the cycle but which must be translated or reinterpreted to man. For this reason, because they are not meant to be subtle, realistic human studies, Jeffers' characters tend to be stereotypes.

Jeffers' men are typically victims. They embody the Apollonian traits of law and order, stability, civilization, permanence, stoic presumptuousness. His women on the other hand are agents of change, violence, and death. Jeffers' women embody Dionysian traits of intuition, revolution, dark destructiveness, mutability. They are agents of the god. Therefore Jeffers' plot patterns tend to be predictable and, it must be confessed, repetitious. Typically they use a family triangle, often an incestuous one, to set up a dynamic of destruction. The plot patterns end in the annihilation which ritually is a means by which the cycle renews itself. Catharsis seldom comes for the protagonist. Instead it comes for the poet and for the readers who watch and are instructed. It is not a purging of emotion but a moving beyond emotion to accept stoically the nature of things, as with Orestes' "tower beyond tragedy." Catharsis means clarification.

Lest the reader miss the myth-ritual and parabolic intent, Jeffers interlaces his narratives with choric interludes which progressively comment on the meaning of the story at the anagogic or mystical level. It is embarrassing to find the critic-commentators on "Roan Stallion," for instance, ignoring entirely the heavy theological explication which the poet offers progressively through the story by means of lyric interpolations like "Humanity is the start of the race . . . ," "The fire threw up figures and symbols . . . ." The poet is saying directly to the reader: this story is meant to shock you out of your narrow religious preoccupations. It is intended to immunize you against the virus of idolatry.

Jeffers' lyric poems are as complex as his narratives are. As lyricist, Jeffers is a poet of many voices. However, the critics have been mostly tone-deaf, and what they have managed to hear they refuse to accept. First of all, Jeffers is preëminently a prophet in the Old Testament mold. He is a voice crying out in the wilderness, a critic and naysayer to the political and social establishment. The prophet, of course, is not known for his softspoken, mannerly, balanced presentations of a point. Instead he shouts to near-deaf ears and writes large for the almost blind. In order to convey truth, he exaggerates. He is harsh in hopes of shocking a few at least into thought and reaction. Therefore it is absurd to chide the prophet for being out of sorts or misanthropic. "Rearmament," "Shine, Republic," and "Sirens" are good examples of Jeffers' prophetic lyrics.

Jeffers is a mystic. He found divinity in the landscape, in the storm, and in the stars. A man of intense piety, he was worshipful of the universe, in love with its cosmic God. He tried to see things from his god's point of view, and that is a view in which man's importance necessarily diminishes. The poems "Night," "Signpost," and "Love the Wild Swan" are striking examples of his mystic ardor. Moreover, Jeffers was an inquisitor, probing the heresies and dogmatic exaggerations of men. He was an iconoclast who saw the idols of religious partisanship and humanistic creeds as blasphemies. His lyric interludes in

"Roan Stallion" carry this message, as does the intensely purifying final speech of Orestes in "The Tower Beyond Tragedy."

Jeffers is an exorcist, attempting with poetic incantations to drive out the evil spirits that blind and benumb, evil spirits which were for him the neurotic obsessions of the human race for centrality, invulnerability, immortality, and immunity. "To the Stone-Cutters," "The Cruel Falcon," "Rock and Hawk," and "The Place for No Story" aim at this exorcism. But Jeffers is also a therapist, endeavoring to lead himself and others to see life as a unity and to accept the conditions of Being, which include pain, death, and personal obliteration, in order to find peace and wisdom in a cosmic context. "Apology For Bad Dreams" appeals for such a re-education.

Jeffers is a philosopher, espousing truth whatever the cost. "Continent's End" seeks ultimate causes, fountains of fire in an oscillating universe. "Theory of Truth" searches out the flaws in religious visions of the past, and "The Truce and the Peace" seeks the seeds of acceptance and serenity within the heart. Going farther, Jeffers is also an apocalyptist. His formula for existence has violence at its core, for Beauty, change, violence, being, and God are interchangable. The world at every level is cyclic and must renew itself through violence.

In some ways, Jeffers is a religious teacher, promulgating Christ-like beatitudes through his lyrics. "Crumbs or the Loaf," as has been noted, clearly proclaims this intent. Likewise he is an ecologist. Long before the word gained popular resonance he spoke of balance, respect, harmonious participation in the ritual processes of nature. Beauty and sanity are part of the integrity of wholeness, as he tells us in "The Answer." Healing comes from re-establishing bonds with the earth, as in "Return" and "Compensation." But above all, Jeffers is a seer. A discovery of the workings of the universe and a deep gratification in their beauty is the hallmark of his *ars poetica*. He felt called to be "a sense organ of god," as in "The Beginning and the End," "His Intelligencer," and "At the Birth of an Age."

Besides functioning in all these capacities, Jeffers is pre-eminently our poet of the West. His poetry establishes a profound identification with the "Continent's End." He draws from the "Drop-off cliff of the world," from the final tide-line, from the headlands towering over the last ocean of immigrations. Here is the metaphysical base for final judgments upon America and the race of men. For on the west coast, the groping, sometimes juvenile, sometimes sadistic, always imperceptive mass has reached a poised moment for decision, facing opposite ways. It faces backward toward its guilts and forward toward its uncertain and beckoning future. These and other "voices" of Jeffers are a stumbling block for many. Such "voices" require a fine-tuned receptiveness that unfortunately is not always attainable. But even to those readers who are only slightly discerning, the distinctions are instructive and the insights rewarding.

Jeffers' poetry, then, is characterized by a total seriousness, with no place for humor, no break in intensity; by confrontations at every turn, including the relentless seeking of crisis themes; by a uniquely-constructed myth system involving re-creations of Agamemnon, Phaedra, Medea and other mythological figures having to do with primal forces in our present; by a preoccupation with cosmic violence, which requires a pacifist, isolationist temperament and which accepts God on his own terms; by a form of character portrayal and plot development that is not primarily realistic, but one which interprets parabolically to man the world of larger-than-man; by a pessimism concerning man's sanity and permanence by an optimism concerning the endurance of beauty and the ongoing experiments of God; by a desire to convert, coupled with a doctrinaire fatalism; and by an angry, anguished, scolding prophetic voice which is set against a resigned, stoic apocalyptic vision.

There is ample reason to speak of Jeffers as a poet of the West *par excellence.* One is tempted to agree that he is *the* poet of the West, as William Everson dubs him in his "Archetype West" essay (*Regional Perspectives,* Chicago, 1973). Jeffers' poetry represents not merely a poetic use of the West but a fathomless identification with it, and especially with its landscape, which was for Jeffers a paradigm by which to understand all existence. A Jeffers volume usually contains a narrative accompanied by a cluster of related lyrics which tend to be epiphanic insights into the theme of the primary work, that is, of the narrative. Located mostly on the slopes of the Coast Range from Monterey to Big Sur, his narratives do not merely seek a backdrop in Western landscape, but they give the landscape voice so that it may speak vatically. Of one of these narratives he says, almost as though he refers to all of them: "The story grows rather intimately from the rock of this coast."

Jeffers tries to "get clear of" the human. "More like the ceremonial dances of primitive people," he says, "the dancer becomes a rain-cloud, or a leopard, or a God. . . . The episodes of the poem are a sort of essential ritual, from which the real action develops on another plane" (*Selected Letters,* No. 65). In that late lyric, "My Loved Subject," he avers, "Mountain and ocean, rock, water and beasts and trees / Are the protagonists, the human people are only symbolic interpreters." His characters, therefore, interpret the Western landscape, making its voice clearer, its lesson more easily perceptible. The West, this new, wild, virtually unconquerable region, its inaccessible mountains, obliterating wilderness, jagged coastal headlands, is for Jeffers the revelation. By its vastness, the West is vigor and violence, untrammeled, untamed, unhuman. It is therefore an unbiased witness, a disinterested spokesman for the universe and its god.

As Jeffers perceives it, the West is an essential revelation of God's life, of man's predicament, of the nature of things. In the famous pivotal lyric entitled "Night," Jeffers despairs of comprehending the galactic and cosmic dimensions in space and time, and so he turns to the Coast Range:

> To us the near-hand mountain
> Be a measure of height, the tide-worn cliff at the sea-
>   gate a measure of continuance.

But this is not any mountain, any seascape. "Apology for Bad Dreams," Jeffers' most complete statement of his artistic intent, asserts that it is precisely this coast alone, America's terminal shore, that demands tragedies, victims, Titans, immolations. Quiet places and less beautiful places demand less, invoke less, communicate less.

"Subjected Earth," the lyric that concludes "Descent to the Dead," which is his poem sequence on Ireland, contrasts the vibrant Western rim of the world with the "soft alien twilight worn and weak" of that European terrain, "so kneaded with human flesh, so humbled and changed."

> I remembered impatiently
> How the long bronze mountain of my own coast,
> Where color is no account and pathos ridiculous,
>   the sculpture is all,
> Breaks the arrows of the setting sun . . .

Having examined the lands of his forefathers, Jeffers is moved to return to his primary task to celebrate his primordial place in the American West:

> The great memory of that unhumanized world,
> With all its wave of good and evil to climb yet,
> Its exorbitant power to match, its heartless passion
>   to equal,
> And all its music to make. . . . (*Selected Poetry*, p. 483)

Flagons and Apples (1912), Jeffers' first volume of poetry, was not Western, nor was it in any way typical of what the poet was yet to do in verse. Printed at his own expense, it received very little critical or popular attention. Its forty-six pages and thirty-three poems are not remarkable except perhaps that in contrast to the later work they seem to be mostly love lyrics of praise, loss, joy, pain, union, and separation. Of these poems it has been said that Jeffers was imitating the English Romantics.

Jeffers' second volume, *Californians* (1916), is transitional in a very uneven way. As William Everson notes in his introduction to the reissue of this volume (1970), "Stephen Brown," "The Vardens," and "The Three Avilas" reveal that the poet, though still uncertain and earthbound, is beginning to work with the dynamics of his coast and with its self-revelatory qualities. Here also he first acknowledges the role of terrain or landscape as genesis or analogue for the plots of his poems:

> The poems [are] . . . closely involved with the nature of the country. The story of the three Avilas, for example, grew up like a plant from the ravine described in it, through which the first stream north of the river flows into Carmel Bay;—the story about Ruth Alison derived from a clump of perfectly albino redwood shoots in Big Sur Valley, from a few people met there, and from the grand and sombre Beauty of that forest. (*Californians*, p. 163)

This insight into his poetic art was one which he was to reiterate throughout his career (see *Selected Letters*, No. 231, in reference to "Thurso's Landing" and his subtitle and preface to *Jeffers Country*).

Coastal landscape is a prime element of Jeffers' *Tamar and Other Poems* (1924). The whole volume is extraordinary. For both the poet and the person Jeffers, it reflects a conversion no less radical than Whitman's as mirrored in *Leaves of Grass*. The title poem is like nothing else in American literature.

"Tamar" takes place on Point Lobos, a rocky knoll and a mini-peninsula jutting into the Pacific across from Carmel, its submerged rocks churning the sea white, and its coves and fissures trapping the tidal ebb and flow, turning the water into hissing geysers and seething cauldrons. Its cypress grove is twisted, worn, and lichen-crusted by the seawinds and coastal storms. To Jeffers, Point Lobos evidently prefigured the ominous violence inherent in all things. Its reverberation was apocalyptic, and Jeffers fills it with spectre horsemen, cups of wrath, storm, quake, deluge, and holocaust. The story examines the coast and the continent's fall-off cliff almost as the ultimate reminder of the fall of man.

Of his Eve-like heroine Jeffers asks: "Was it the wild coast / Of her breeding, and the reckless wind / In the beaten trees and the gaunt booming crashes / Of breakers under the rocks, or rather the amplitude / And wing-subduing immense earth-ending water / That moves all the west taught her this freedom?" Tamar's annihilative vision-dream (*Selected Poetry,* p. 17) views the coast as terminus of the race. The universal music calls each wave of immigrants—Indians, Spaniards, English-speaking—as though the immigrants were lemmings drawn to the final obliteration of the wide water. Tamar's father envisions the coast cliff as a "lookout" from which to witness an imminent holocaust: "I have prayed to the hills to come and cover me, / We are on the drop-off cliff of the world and dare not meet Him, I with two days to live, even I / Shall watch the ocean boiling and the sea curl up like paper in a fire and the dry bed / Crack to the bottom." Yet another focal point for "Tamar" is the tide-line, which has special significance in all of Jeffers' work. To Jeffers, the tide-line is a no-man's-land between life and death, between new hopes and old guilts, between human and non-human presences. Again, it is not any tide-line but the one at the end of the whole pilgrimage of Western civilization.

24

In mere plot-summary, Jeffers' story of brother-sister incest can easily fall victim to parody. "Tamar" is actually Jeffers' masterpiece, an intricate working of the mythic, ritual, and religious pattern with profound revelatory significance for the human spirit. Tamar was the biblical daughter of David, raped by one brother and avenged by another, the incident signaling civil war and almost the downfall of the Davidic monarchy. In the Canaanite religion, Tamar is the fertility goddess, the earthmother, who acts in the final seasonal phase as executioner and as savior of her brother consort.

Jeffers uses the mythic levels, with their rituals of sexual initiation which prefigure death, of descent and devolution as in Tamar's beach dance, and of purgation by fire, to confront a Luther-like vision of predestination and depravity. To the overriding question, Where does peace lie? Jeffers answers: in radical innocence. Tamar, operating as an agent of God who is the "breaker of trees," reaches an innocence beyond despair by detaching herself and by observing the scene of her perverse actions as though from a mountain in Asia or from the Morning Star. Tamar's sin begins a Nietzschean transvaluation of values in which freedom is redefined as the ability to perceive and accept, in which peace is redefined as the integrity gained by perspective and annulled hope, and in which the evils of corruption, incest, and holocaust are redefined as the necessary down-swing of the cycle.

Jeffers appears to be writing himself a parable to quiet psychic disturbances that arise from a sense of inner perversity, as in Paul's conflicting laws—Romans 7:15—or from concern with the world's dissolution. Jeffers' story works on at least three levels: the fall of the house of Cauldwell, the fall of Western civilization as prefigured in World War I, and the end of life on the planet, as in David's vision of the seas boiling. The lesson taught is that these three are different faces of the same reality. They are inevitable. They have nothing to do with personal peace.

"Tamar" is accompanied by a shorter narrative, "The Coast-Range Christ," which follows the career of a war resister against a mythic pattern recalling both Jesus and the year-god. The terrain is again the Carmel river mouth. David Carrow is a personification of the Christian age, ineffectual and self-immolating in its futile search for peace.

Of the lyrics that accompany the *Tamar* volume, "Point Pinos and Point Lobos" and "Point Joe" comment on the sacral quality of the serrated stone's primitive beauty that both dwarfs and instructs mankind. In order to express the inter-play of war-turbulence and disillusioned love within himself, Jeffers revisits in "Mal Paso Bridge" the place where Tamar and Lee fell from grace. "Natural Music" overhears the contrasting water sounds at the Carmel river mouth and reconciles the poet to famine, war, and the fall of cities. "Salmon-Fishing" relates the solstice rite at the river mouth to the sacrificial impulse throughout the life span of the human race. Three poems commemorating the artist's building of Tor House relate the poet's life to the rock of the final coast. In these poems, the essence of that rock instructs his poetry. "Continent's End" reflects Jeffers' concern with establishing identity within a space-time continuum. At spring equinox, in a quiet moment of reassessment, he feels the American continent under his feet and ponders the Pacific, the beginning and end of human migrations. His conclusion shifts from the evolutionary cycle of the earth to the cycle of the universe. Then Jeffers invokes the "tides of fire" which are the beginning and the end of all migrations, even those of the stars.

Roan Stallion (1925) was a quick follow-up and an extension of the *Tamar* poems. The title narrative takes a young quarter-breed woman named California through a series of sacramental rites on the final coast, where Jeffers' God reclaims the poet's religious myths and reaffirms his incarnation. Having undergone a baptismal transformation in a midnight Carmel River crossing, California goes to her nuptials atop the dome of coastal hills beyond Robinson Canyon with the "savage and exultant strength of the world," the stallion. The poem is about the mystic experience. It celebrates the wild god of the universe as he breaks through human awareness in theophany. As parable, the story is a plea for openness to a god self-revealed at certain moments in power and beauty. This plea runs counter to the entire religious history of the human race, which relentlessly makes idols out of the vehicles of divine revelation, be they Christ, Lao, Buddha, or stallion.

The second narrative of this volume, "The Tower Beyond Tragedy," recreates the Oresteia trilogy of Aeschylus. The seacoast is Mycenae in ancient Greece, but the symbols are those of Jeffers' coast: stone, mountain, sea cataract, wave, pine forest. As parable, the story embodies the dilemma of family and dynasty power-lust. Orestes, one of Jeffers' pure heroes, finds peace by withdrawing from incestuous human patterns to become one with the mountain.

The lyrics in *Roan Stallion* again make use of the Pacific headlands, of the granite and cypress, the gulls and herons, the clouds and sunsets, the sea vistas and canyon recesses. Each seeks to put man into a context of geologic time and seasonal cycle which dwarfs, humbles, and sanctifies him. The pivotal poem, "Night," takes the poet from seascape, tides, and tower to astronomic time and space in order to reconcile him to life and death, and in order to show him the divinity of the whole. "Shine, Perishing Republic" looks eastward upon a nation that is in the Spenglerian down-cycle. It recalls that the natural process requires decay of nations as much as of orchard fruit, and it attempts to disentangle the corruptive process from feelings of blame or regret. At the same time, the poet urges withdrawal to the mountains, saying that "corruption never has been compulsory." Such imagery is highly suggestive of Christ's eschatological discourse in Matthew 25. "The Torch-Bearers Race" calls for a new dream, a new direction, a new frontier now that the last ocean has been reached. The poet envisions the colonizing of the stars, with the life-force passing from man to a new form of life. He seeks new wildernesses ever outward, throwing off the incestuous self-regard that has vitiated the journey to this point.

"Apology for Bad Dreams" is perhaps the most significant of the shorter poems, presenting as it does Jeffers' first full defense of his poetic mode. It begins from a Pacific scene typical of his poems: unbridled beauty of headlands, sea, and sunset. The scene is an epiphany, clouded for a moment by human sadism in the image of a woman torturing an animal. Jeffers reconciles man's cruelty with the world's beauty in a ritualistic manner, by the gestures, the dynamics, the sacrificial implications of both the coastal beauty and the woman's cruelty, which are the same. Distancing is the key. Jeffers explains that he writes poetry lest he become a victim or an agent of blind violence: "Better invent than suffer." The coast, apotheosis of Beauty, instructs him in that violence. Pain, even cruelty, is essential to being, and it must be confronted and affirmed. The world's god tortures himself in all things to discover himself. The poet gives God a new realm of discovery by his invention of paper victims.

The Women at Point Sur (1927), which Jeffers suggested was to be the "Faust for its age," is set in the countryside fifty miles below the poet's stone house and tower. Barclay, its apostate minister protagonist, has left his church to find a god he can truly believe in. In the process of leaping walls and breaking out of humanity (see the choric passage "Humanity is the start of the race" in "Roan Stallion" and repeated here in the "Prelude"), Barclay is self-deceived into gathering disciples. In a monomanic parody of Nietzschean transvaluation, he finally rapes his own daughter and then wanders mad into the mountains to die in bewilderment. The poem dramatizes the axiom of "Apology for Bad Dreams," which declares that the intensity of being induces violence and insanity. Barclay had chosen the wild landscape because "The American mind short-circuits by ignoring its object / Something in the gelded air of the country," but "God thinks through action / And all this show is God's brain, the water, the cloud yonder, the coastal hills, thinking the thing out to conclusion." The minister's quest is honest—to know God and to find the good life—but his means are not pure. The story is choked with sexual inversion, infant sacrifice, compulsion, and hysteria. Jeffers considered it his best effort, but so far the critics have only been struck dumb. The length of the poem precluded the addition of any shorter poems to the volume.

Cawdor (1928) looks south again along the coast to a point half the way to Sur, where headlands tower over a rounded ocean and where vast distances of mountain and crenelated canyon make of the islands of arable land and cattle-forage natural sanctuaries against the incursions of civilization. Jeffers' narrative takes the reader into that wilderness and to a ranch that is sufficient unto itself. This is a sanctuary which ought to insure peace and integrity but which instead becomes the arena of human jealousy and self-destructiveness. At the level of parable, Jeffers seems to be probing this question: Where do integrity and self-possession truly lie? His protagonist, Cawdor, is one of the poet's truly noble characters, but the character has a flaw. In his declining years, after purging himself of the usual lusts for power and possession, he has been lulled into complacency by his geographic invulnerability. Grasping for renewed youth, he marries an indigent young girl who has sought refuge on his ranch.

In a re-enactment of the Phaedra-Hippolytus-Theseus triangle, Cawdor kills his innocent son in a rage of jealously. He then painfully works out his "salvation" by confronting his guilt, by refusing all dishonest ways of psychic escape, and at last by gouging out his eyes in expiation for the pride and lust which have blinded him spiritually. The plot illustrates the truth that mere relationship to the land does not save. Only a salutary internalizing of the land's indifference and invulnerability can provide salvation.

The narrative is accompanied by lyrics which function as variations on the theme. The titles, "The Summit Redwood," "Ascent to the Sierras," "Bixby's Landing," attest to Jeffers' closeness to the coastal scene and to his transmutation of coastal images into symbols of salvation. "Tor House" offers an example of the depth of Jeffers' commitment to the Western landscape. In fantasy his mind ranges ahead to a post-apocalyptic time when man's present marks on the terrain are obliterated. He locates his beloved house by means of geologic coordinates of granite seashelf and valley floor, of river mouth and bay, saying that if ghosts can haunt a land, his spirit will be here, "deep in the granite."

In a three-page narrative, "A Redeemer," Jeffers proves that the coastal landscape is not merely the final frontier and ultimate vantage point. It is also a "judgment seat" from which to pronounce the verdict on the history of America's Westward migration. Half identifying with his protagonist's tortured consciousness, which wants to avert the vengeance that is due the post-frontier society, Jeffers pictures a half-mad isolate who pierces his hands, making perpetual wounds to atone for the crimes and irreverences of America's "pioneers."

> They have done what never was done before. Not as a
> people takes a land to love it and be fed,
> A little, according to need and love, and again a
> little; sparing the country tribes, mixing

Their blood with theirs, their minds with all the
    rocks and rivers, their flesh with the soil; no,
    without hunger
Wasting the world and your own labor, without love
    possessing, not even your hands to the dirt but plows
Like blades of knives; heartless machines; houses of steel;
    using and despising the patient earth . . .
Oh, as a rich man eats a forest for profit and a field
    for vanity, so you came west and raped
The continent and brushed its people to death. Without
    need, the weak skirmishing hunters, and without mercy.
Well God's a scarecrow; no vengeance out of old rages.
    But there are acts breeding their own reversals
In their own bellies from the first day. (*Selected Poetry,*
    p. 190)

A second short narrative, "An Artist," presents another half-mad hermit who in the secrecy of his sandstone quarry carves warped, giant figures, "the mould of some ideal humanity that might be worthy to *be* / Under that lighting," tortured because "peace marrying pain alone can breed that excellence in the luckless race, might make it decent." The last poem in *Cawdor,* and one which has been much anthologized but little understood, is "Hurt Hawks." This poem celebrates the poet's totem animal, which reveals in itself the wild god of the world, intemperate and savage. For all its shock-value, the poem is merely an early statement of Jeffers' "inhumanism," proclaimed through the prophet's voice. Its controversial line, "I'd rather, except the penalties, kill a man than a hawk," parallels Jesus' prophetic hyperboles such as "Unless you hate your father and mother and your own life, you cannot be my disciples" (Luke 14:26). In killing a helplessly crippled bird, Jeffers has experienced an epiphany.

Dear Judas (1929) takes its title from Jeffers' single attempt at a Noh play, which probes the mystery of Jesus' personal motives and the phenomenon of his "possession" of 2000 years of history. Its companion piece, "The Loving Shepherdess," projects mankind's ultimate journey into oblivion, dramatizing it upon the coastal mountains which are the last frontier in the long migration of civilization. A sensitive, mad, forlornly-doomed girl dies in childbirth after her compulsive northering pilgrimage from her father's coastal sheep ranch below Sur to the San Joaquin Valley.

> Walking with numbed and cut feet
> Along the last ridge of migration
> On the last coast above the not-to-be-colonized
> Ocean, across the streams of the people
> Drawing a faint pilgrimage
> As if you were drawing a line at the end of the world
> Under the columns of ancestral figures:
> So many generations in Asia,
> So many in Europe, so many in America:
> To sum the whole. (*Selected Poetry*, pp. 229-30)

Re-enacting in an inverted fashion the Good Shepherd parable, Clare Walker proves the futility of saviorism. Rather than leading her sheep to safety, she brings them to death one by one. A doomed Christ-figure, ridiculed, refused comfort, forsaken, without a place to lay her head, doomed to an April agony and death, she sees her fate prefigured in the salmon migration, which is a living parable for her instruction. Though she has broken out of humanity to love all things, her love is still not pure enough, since it has been caught up in sentimentality.

On her pilgrim's way Clare is sometimes accompanied by Onorio Vasquez, a simple-minded vaquero mystic, who sees true visions but who never understands them. He sees his ancestors, the ancient Aztecs and Mayans, whose migrations had coursed down this coast. He has visions that reveal the cosmos to be a homogeneity of energy which is simultaneously of one substance with darkness. The vaquero mystic also sees good and evil eternally balanced, and he sees inexhaustible fountains feeding "the great rivers of the blood of life." In his last vision Onorio meets Christ on the road, as St. Peter did in the *Quo Vadis* legend. Christ chides Onorio: "If I go to Calvary ten million times: what is that to you / Let me go up." The Christ in this vision is the cycle god, agonized in each and all, seeking new ways to suffer. It is a Dionysian figure rather than the Orthodox Christ. His message is one of fatality.

The *Dear Judas* volume closes with three touching meditations on Western vistas. ' 'Evening Ebb" glories in the birds, the tide, and the star of a perfect Pacific evening. "Hands" lets prehistoric people speak from cave marks near Tassajara Springs, saying "All will pass." "Hooded Night" overlooks the fog-breathing ocean, the rock, and the cypress, and the poem declares that these things are the lasting reality. This dark glory tells man of his mortality.

Thurso's Landing (1952) begins with the title poem, which again pronounces doom for the Westering movement that has been so recently completed. Thurso's coastal family is, as it were, on the prow of a ship, but it is a ship foundering in its journey toward the last rock shore of oblivion. Much as in "Tamar," the throes of the protagonist foreshadow the wreck of the race. With the sails set, the ballast heavy, Jeffers asks how should men live? what is man's place? where is his dignity? The final lines of "Thurso's Landing" provide a striking summary. Reave Thurso, brought low for his *hubris* in desiring to blot out the failures of his ancestry, and having endured excruciating, continuous pain, at last allows his wife to take him to a high cliff overlooking the Pacific in the midst of storm. There he dies in stoic dignity:

The platform is like a rough plank theatre-stage
Built on the brow of the promontory: as if our blood had
    labored all around the earth from Asia
To play its mystery before strict judges at last, the
    final ocean and sky, to prove our nature
More shining than that of the other animals. It is
    rather ignoble in its quiet times, mean in its pleasures,
Slavish in the mass; but at stricken moments it can shine
    terribly against the dark magnificence of things.

Once again the lyrics of this volume celebrate the coastal intensity of Jeffers' environs. "The Place for No Story" admires the mystical beauty of an area unaffected as yet by any human migration, unneedful of man for its glory, and existing outside man's life. The coast ranchers' annual ritual of burning pasture lands for a new grass crop becomes the focal point for a haunting, excruciating reconciliation with pain and terror in "Fire on the Hills." "November Surf" considers the polluting presence of the recent intruder, man. The last sea-cliff of the frontier, littered with "Wonderbread" wrappers and condoms, awaits the deluge by which in one mighty surge the Pacific will cleanse the "cumbered" continent. "Winged Rock" is a simple, appreciative description of the birds that are the "imagination" of Tor House—pigeons, kildeer, finches, gulls, and hawks. "The Bed by the Window" contemplates Jeffers' guest room bed, which overlooks the Western shore fifty yards below, and which takes into its vista the Carmel River mouth, the steep-banked beach, and the pine and cypress forest of Point Lobos. This was the deathbed for both Una and Robinson Jeffers. In this lyric, death is foreseen from a distance of thirty years, balancing against death in perfect indifference.

The two non-California poems of the volume are instructive. Reflecting upon Jeffers' visit to Tony and Mabel Luhan in Taos, "New Mexican Mountain" pictures tourist-America sucking the vitality from the Indian religious forms, here the rain or corn dance. "Second-Best" reviews Jeffers' bloody Saxon ancestry in order to suggest that he may be living life second-hand. He responds with a reaffirmation of his vocation: the apocalyptic angel comes and requires poetry of him.

The last short narrative, "Margrave," begins with a lyric prelude in which the poet re-establishes his essential stance on the Western Shore. It is as though Jeffers must first locate his true geographic and astronomic position in order to write a poem, any poem. Climbing the forty-foot stone tower, built with his own hands of sea boulders, the poet grasps the parapet until he senses the reeling of the universe. He feels the thrust of the earth below him in its spin, the momentum of the planet in its solar orbit, the movement of the solar system in its galactic swing, and finally the centrifugal dispersal of galaxies. The continent's end points him heavenward. The story itself is about the megalomania of a youth convicted of kidnapping and murder. He had committed these crimes in order to subsidize his medical career. Amidst hysteria and morbid ruminations, he ponders the loss that the race will sustain when it is deprived of his genius. Jeffers locates reconciliation in the need for God to dream bad dreams as well as good.

Give Your Heart to the Hawks (1935) opens with a hundred-page narrative debating the social obligations incurred by blood-guilt. In artful recreations of the Garden of Eden and the Cain and Abel stories, Jeffers follows the terrible regret-pangs and escape strategies of a fratricide, Lance Frazer. Though dubiously motivated, Lance's wife, Fayne, offers her husband a salvation. For whatever punishment is due, he must give his heart to the god of nature, but not to men, nor to their legal system, nor to their prisons. But Lance cannot be Prometheus, shackled to the Western mountain of his crime and eaten by the vulture of self-recrimination. He goes mad, and during a headlong escape south along the rim of the world, he hurls himself, scapegoat-fashion, onto the sea rocks.

The lyrics of this volume are more abstract than earlier ones, and they look distantly toward a new world war brewing in the sick attitudes of the age. "A Little Scraping" compares the times to a bad plastering job which can be demolished in a shower of chips and sand to reveal what is real and enduring. Under the plaster, the things of permanence are the mountainous sea-coast, which is part of the great and timeless excellence of things, and God, "secretly smiling, the beautiful power / That piles up cities for the poem of their fall." The lyric "Intellectuals" deplores the follower-syndrome among those who should lead the world. "Triad" puts aside Marxism and science and exalts the poet whose business is to "awake dangerous images and call the hawks." "Still the Mind Smiles" commemorates a kind of Blakeian "Marriage of Heaven and Hell." In the larger context Jeffers sees that excesses—civilization and squalid savagery, war and peace—balance each other. They reveal the "splendor of God, the exact poet." "Crumbs or the Loaf," a brief manifesto of sorts, proposes to insinuate bitter truths by parable.

The lyric section of the volume closes with a gathering of Irish poems which Jeffers wrote during a trip to Britain in 1929 and which he published in a limited edition of 500 copies in 1931 as *Descent to the Dead*. These poems confirm Jeffers as poet of the Pacific. In his imagination he has descended into his ancestral and racial past. There he finds dynamism and intensity of life in the grave mounds of dead heroes, but he believes that the European continent is worn out. Its landscape is too covered with human remains. It is unrevelatory, and it needs to recover its inherent divinity, whereas his own shore beckons, as he says in the last poem "Subjected Earth."

Solstice (1935) launches Jeffers in earnest upon his World War phase. A "solstice" is a standing still. Here it is the low point of the solar cycle. "At the Birth of An Age," the verse drama which opens the volume, examines the beginnings of the Christian era in the tensions generated between Eastern or Christian religion and Western or Germanic heroic blood. In the preface which Jeffers wrote for the poem, he explains his interest in the dynamics which have sustained the culture-age for two thousand years, and his interest in the processes that now mark its decline. These processes are the fading of Christian faith into a Utopian ethic and "the physical and especially the spiritual hybridization that civilized life always brings with it." The impending war is a sign of this enervation, this downward momentum of the cycle. The war is inevitable, and Jeffers must reconcile himself. "I would burn my right hand in a slow fire / To change the future . . . I should do foolishly," he says. In "Rearmament" he attempts to see beauty in the disastrous rhythm of war preparations. The lyric "What are Cities For?" yields the terrible answer: they are for beautiful agonies. "Ave Caesar," "Shine, Republic," "The Trap," each abhors the sheeplike apathy which turns over vigilance and freedom for softness, irresponsibility, and self-blinding.

Other poems seek symbols in nature for the wisdom which is necessary if one is to endure the coming storm. "The Cruel Falcon" urges fierce, hard values against the false security that destroys men's souls. "Rock and Hawk" exalts the best of animate and inanimate worlds—fierce realism and mystic disinterestedness. "Life from the Lifeless" acknowledges the primary beauty of inanimate things. "Gray Weather" creates a mood of deep meditation in the lull between violences. "Signpost," one of Jeffers' best lyrics, suggests that the only way to love man is to climb "Jacob's ladder" from the pit of self out to the stars and then to look back at the incredibly dwarfed context of human endeavor and concern. "Love the Wild Swan" assures Jeffers that not even his own poetry matters. All that really matters is the wild beauty of the world, which is invulnerable, ineffable, and divine. "Return" calls for a purging of distractions and a healing immersion in earth. "Flight of Swans" locates the poet's gift in seeing things as they are.

The title poem, "Solstice," 'is a modernized "Medea" in which primitive power and earth-wisdom is pitted against rationalizing, homocentric civilization. Madrone Bothwell, modern counterpart of the witch of Colchis, slays her children and buries them in the coast range lest her husband civilize them in the degrading, urban maze. Bothwell represents the Apollonian world, and Madrone represents the Dionysian retribution which inevitably must visit such a world. A parable for the age, this solstice is the stagnation point, a fateful standing still, the wave cresting and about to fall. It is the sacrificial turn of the season which is pictured in "Salmon-Fishing." Here the victim is not a migrating salt-water fish. Instead, it is the culture-age.

Such Counsel You Gave To Me (1937) reiterates themes and symbols of the *Solstice* volume. The war is closing fast, and the turbulent title poem personifies and dramatizes the split mind of modern civilization. An idealistic, abstracted young man returns from medical school on the edge of breakdown and kills his earthbound father while battling an incestuous attraction toward his young mother. Incest again bespeaks introverted man's inability to break out of human solipsism.

The lyrics in this volume return to the poet's anxiety over the war and over the sickness of civilization. Some seek alternative life directions. "The Coast-Road," "Going to Horse Flats," and "The Wind-Struck Music" celebrate the simple life, a life that is removed from the world's self-centered agonies, a life of herdsmen and hermits, a life that is timeless and that is somehow outside the cycle of civilization. Therefore it is a wiser life as well. Other poems grapple with the Dionysian downhill career of the West. "The Purse-Seine" likens the cities to the sardine catches which shine in frantic agitation as the net closes. "Blind Horses" and "Thebaid" look to the syndromes of power and escapist faith which have given the times over to imperialism, a sign of the end. "The Answer" offers stoicism, detachment, and love of the divine-whole as salvation. "New Year's Eve" and "Hope is Not for the Wise" lay Jeffers' fear of tyrants, luxury, and war at rest in that larger context of beauty.

"Oh Lovely Rock" and "Beaks of Eagles" reach the same peace-giving perspective—through the relativity of time. "Nova" gains comfort in ultimate astronomic cataclysm (death-throes of our sun) that makes miniscule our smaller violences. In "Night Without Sleep" the poet reminds himself of the ultimate integration of man with nature. The wounds of war will heal just as the wooded mountainside, torn by landslide, will be healed. Here too Jeffers pauses to question his own motives in writing; "Self-Criticism in February" answers the critics of his gloom. His defense is that of the prophet, rejected but true to his vision and to his God.

The Selected Poetry of Robinson Jeffers (1938) is a collection of most of these works, but it omits a lyric here and there, and it omits several of the long narratives for want of space. It concludes with a section of four "New Poems and Fragments," the most significant of which is a philosophical meditation, "Theory of Truth," which asks why so few seek truth and why the most intense seekers — Jesus, Lao, Buddha — characteristically are caught up in impurities which warp their conclusions. Jeffers concludes that the search for truth is foredoomed and frustrated "until the mind has turned its love from itself and man, from parts to the whole."

Jeffers published four more volumes of poems in his lifetime. The first two remained enmeshed in the war's onrush and aftermath. The third adapted an ancient play to Judith Anderson's dramatic genius. The fourth attempted to deal with his wife's death.

Be Angry at the Sun (1941) takes its title from a lyric rather than from a narrative, and its admonition attempts to take the sting out of "corruption, empire, war." "Mara," the first narrative, retains the husband-wife-brother triangle which is familiar in Jeffers' plot-patterns. Mara, who represents bitterness, functions as doppelgänger for Bruce Fergusson, a "deceived and jealous man / who bawled for the truth, the truth, and failed to endure / Its first gleam." He is a man who as Jeffers confesses in the lyric "For Una," is in "some ways / My very self but mostly an antipodes." At the parabolic level, the poem exposes the public self-deception and cowardice that makes suicide the only solution for Western man.

"Bowl of Blood" is a masque in which Hitler is visited by Frederick the Great and Napoleon. Hitler is misled by a prophecy of his youthful friend Friedenau, and so he prolongs the war and increases the bloodshed. The poem attempts to present a strategy for stoically accepting the war: "Power has the man." The tragic fall must be worked through to its final act. The "old rotten tree," a symbol of the past-ripe civilization, will be "justified by a sprouting acorn," representing renewal. For the most part, the lyrics of the volume reiterate this theme. They deal with the inevitability of cultural collapse as set forth in the Spenglerian thesis, with the poet's role in storing wisdom for the future while remaining unentangled, and with the beauty of destruction. Some of the lyrics consider America's death-wish as expressed in luxuries, distractions, and opiates. Jeffers also expresses his own despair for ideologies and his religious awe at the fall of nations and civilizations. Admittedly Jeffers is here caught in repetition and self-parody. Few of the poems are memorable. "The Day is a Poem," "Contemplation of the Sword," and "The Bloody Sire" are perhaps the best, each seizing upon some violence and extracting its beauty.

Medea (1946) is refreshingly non-topical. Writing at the request of Judith Anderson, Jeffers adapted Euripides' play in masterly fashion. The stage production was excruciating in its intensity, inspiring terror and a certain exaltation in Medea's triumph. The underlying theme restates a familiar parabolic lesson: Apollonian power and arrogance are foredoomed by Dionysian earth forces which restore balance and close the cycle. The lesson is instructive, but thankfully, it maintains a distance between itself and post-war politics.

The Double Axe (1948) completes Jeffers' war-obsessed poems —without achieving the distance and peace repeatedly advocated therein. The "double axe" is the two-edged sword of Revelations, the ankh, ancient symbol of generation, the cross. The title here joins two narratives. The first, "The Love and the Hate," presents a young American soldier who is a casualty of the Pacific war. He is resurrected from an island grave by his sheer hatred of his father's American Legion chauvinism, which had first convinced him to enlist and then had sacrificed him. He returns to his parental ranch in California to execute both his father and his mother's young lover, leaving her to commit suicide following a fire that blackens the land. This apocalyptic consummation sets the stage for the second drama, "The Inhumanist," This is the story of the caretaker at the Gore ranch who personifies Jeffers' inhumanist ideal, a hermit of the Western shore who is recognized as seer but who rejects disciples.

Except perhaps for two or three, the shorter poems of this volume are too strident and war-immersed to be enduring. "Cassandra" acknowledges the bitter frustration in the prophetic stance. "Advice to Pilgrims" urges extrication from immortality-vendors, demagogues, and those who need love. "Original Sin" imagines the beginnings of human cruelty in a mastodon's death by fire.

Hungerfield and Other Poems (1952-54), Jeffers' last work, returns to the old, less topical subject matter, and to the scenes of the coast which he had largely abandoned in the previous two volumes. The title poem is clearly a parable by which Jeffers would exorcise his tearing desire to have his Una back from the dead. In an agonized lyric frame for the story, he relives the year that has passed since her death. With more vigor than wisdom, Hungerfield, his hero, has fended off Death from his mother, and in doing so he has disastrously interfered in the natural process. In defying nature, Hungerfield makes himself a monster, precipitates the deaths of his innocent wife and child, kills his brother, and burns down his house.

"Carmel Point," "Morro Bay," "Ocean," "Skunks," "The Old Stonemason," "The Deer Lay Down Their Bones"—each poem distills from the place, the far Pacific shore, a wisdom to be pondered. "Carmel Point" reiterates the "frontiersman-as-spoiler" motif, noting that the pristine beauty is now defaced with a crop of suburban houses, but that beauty "lives in the very grain of the granite" and awaits human demise. "De Rerum Virtute," a long philosophical meditation, reasserts reluctantly the beauty of man, recognizable only because it is part of the whole: all is intended, all is good and full of God.

In the course of Jeffers' career, covering forty-three years, he offered to the world twenty books of verse. A year after his death, Random House released *The Beginning and the End* (1963) a collection of forty-five hitherto unpublished poems and three uncollected pieces which Jeffers may or may not have wanted to see light. During Jeffers' last days his faithful friend, biographer, and sometimes unofficial editor, Melba Bennett, took on the task of gathering, typing, reviewing, and readying for publication poems of the waning years. According to Mrs. Bennett, Jeffers reluctantly cooperated. Almost blind, depleted of energies by chronic illness, and incapable of long concentration, he suggested that she make the decisions. He sent her a sheaf of revised manuscripts, but then he was unable to make any decision on what should be published.

The Beginning and the End is an uncertain conglomeration, gathered under these headings: The Roots of All Things, Do You Still Make War?, Memoranda, Autobiographical, and Three

Uncollected Poems. The poems, all lyrics, have their fascination, and they give a needed last word by the poet on many of the themes with which he had worked in unresolved tension throughout his career. The title poem is a *tour de force,* a recapitulation of the life of the earth through evolution, from amino acids to the emergence of the "ground ape." The concluding lines give a surprising if still hesitant tribute to man's role in the universe: "The human race is one of God's sense organs. . . . He might go far / And end in honor. The hawks are more heroic but man has a steeper mind, / Huge pits of darkness, high points of light. / You may calculate a comet's orbit or the dive of a hawk, not a man's mind."

"The Great Explosion" uses as metaphor the eighty-billion-year cycle of the "oscillating universe" in order to describe God's heartbeat and pulse. Man's violence and upheaval are a homesickness "for the howling fire-blast that we were born from"; it is all part of God's life. "The Great Wound" explores man's use of myths—scientific, political, religious, and poetic, each alongside truth but never touching it. "He is All" pictures God as an old Basque shepherd talking to himself, having wild fantasies but being a great poet. "But I Am Growing Old and Indolent" revisits "Apology for Bad Dreams," quoting five lines from its second strophe: "Make sacrifices once a year to magic / Horror away from the house. . . ." The aged Jeffers regrets that he did not keep that resolve but does not clarify the salvific effect that such horror stories were meant to have. He does not say whether they were self-educative only, or therapy for internal violences, or a ritual participation by which he moved closer to God.

The poems as a whole are useful as late statements upon man's value and upon his future, as application of old views to new problems like the atomic war, the population explosion, and the cold war. They are useful also as evidence that Jeffers had no startling changes or conversions late in life. The late poems, for their philosophic backdrop, could be part of the *Tamar* volume. But they are repetitious, many are close to prose, some are obscure and faltering. They cover Jeffers' spectrum of themes: God and man, beauty of place, human self-distinction, hazards to the poet, endemic cruelty, omens of disaster, the need for distance and indifference, reconciliation with violence, the future of his family, desire for death, deflation under the stars.

As is the case with most poets, unpublished Jeffers poems will occasionally continue to appear singly or in collected volumes They appear without his authority, and often despite his prior disavowal of their worthiness. Recent examples are *The Alpine Christ and Other Poems* and *Brides of the South Wind,* both by Cayucos Press, edited and carefully assessed by William Everson, early disciple of Jeffers and poet in his own right. Everson explains in his preface to *Californians*—which Cayucos Press has reprinted, along with *Flagons and Apples*—that one takes the extraordinary and presumptuous step in editing and printing poems rejected by the author only for grave and compelling reasons. The reasons are that the rejected poems give scholars a means of tracing the development of the artist. These poems call for no comment here. They and others like them, still in manuscript, represent research materials.

This, then, is Robinson Jeffers, Metaphysician of the Continent's End. When one reviews the spectrum of the themes and modes of literature of the West, one sees that Jeffers came to grips with them all. He dealt with agrarian and pastoral types, the epic sweep, hero archetypes, violence, search for Eden, disaster of the American Dream, Indian extermination, land and landscape, mysticism of wilderness, immersion in nature, onset of progress, and the moral dilemmas of ownership, development, law, power, and greed. His focus is that of a consciously Western writer. The grandson of an early pioneer of Ohio, and the descendent of pre-revolutionary stock, he was always involved in our historical process and in judgment upon it.

There is a deep-seated ambivalence in his poetry. The ambivalence arises from the clash between mystic and prophet. On the one hand, he espouses an Oriental kind of passivity and peace which assumes that nothing can be done. Violence, rape, betrayal, and corruption are variations of a natural process of decay that inevitably follows the cresting of vitality and idealism. This process is totally unblameworthy. On the other hand, Jeffers is an idealistic prophet who has faint hopes that all could be changed. Though he abjured the savior syndrome, in many ways he is the redeemer whom he pictures in the short narrative of that title. His consciousness was raw with the guilts of his people, and he sometimes hoped that through story parables and didactic lyrics he might help to expiate the sins of the people. Jeffers was a continent and three centuries distant from his New England forebears; yet he can be seen as the last puritan on the last coast awaiting the "Day of the Lord."

Elements of Jeffers' poetry may put off the reader, but if one grants the poet his overall view and the genres he carefully chose, the elements fall into place within the whole. He is violent, but so, he would say, is the West; so is existence itself. He is fatalistic. All life, he might answer, having reached the end of its frontier, is aimed at a fall. He is pessimistic, but only in light of the false demand that man should have a permanent place on earth, that man should be central in the universe. He is morbid at times, but there is much in man's history to be morbid about. He exaggerates, which is, of course, the prerogative of the prophet. Hyperbole is his tool to shock, outrage, and move.

Whatever the final judgment on this giant of the Pacific frontier, he presents a poetic and philosophic mind to be reckoned with. A recent survey of criticism on Jeffers (Vardamis, *The Critical Reputation of Robinson Jeffers,* 1972) reveals how awkward and how far from the point have been his commentators thus far. In very recent years there have been signs of a vigorous Jeffers renaissance. The 1960's produced an average of one thoughtful study a year, each one tentatively assessing the poet's life, his philosophical base, and his poetic mode. A biography came forth in 1966. His *Selected Letters* followed in 1968, a prize-winning volume and an essential tool. In 1965 the Sierra Club chose Jeffers' poetry to comment on a magnificent selection of photos of the Big Sur Coast. The title of the book, *Not Man Apart,* comes from Jeffers' poem "The Answer." In 1970, *Jeffers Country,* a volume which the poet himself had planned with a photographer friend, Horace Lyon, reasserted and affirmed his connection with the land.

Caught as he is between time and eternity, between human history and cosmic perspective, Jeffers is difficult to assess. He strove ever to keep his viewpoint as though from the far stars; yet he found himself embroiled in political poetry and in a guilt-ridden American identity. He espoused pacificism and stoic acceptance; yet he was ever driven to analyze and agonize as though holding himself responsible. He based his peace in a philosophy of inhumanism, and at times he seemed to reject not only American life but the life of the whole race as well. Yet he was ever conscious of his roots, of his peculiar human need to reflect upon human existence, and of his compulsion to discover new meaning for his people. He is a poet of the West, therefore, in a very extended sense. He saw the Westering experience as an exemplar of all journeys, geographic and psychological.

Western motifs, as they are usually understood, gave him vehicles for larger philosophizing. The Western continent's edge was to him the divinity of the cosmos revealing itself in measureable lineaments. It is vital, inhospitable, young, violent, full of pain, a stage set for tragedy.

Selected Bibliography

MAJOR WORKS OF ROBINSON JEFFERS

POETRY

Flagons and Apples. Los Angeles: Grafton, 1912.

Californians. New York: Macmillan, 1916.

Tamar and Other Poems. New York: Peter Boyle, 1924.

Roan Stallion, Tamar and Other Poems New York: Boni and Liveright, 1925.

The Women at Point Sur. New York: Liveright, 1927.

Cawdor and Other Poems. New York: Liveright, 1928.

Dear Judas and Other Poems. New York: Liveright, 1929.

Thurso's Landing and Other Poems. New York: Liveright, 1932.

Give Your Heart to the Hawks and Other Poems. New York: Random House, 1933.

Solstice and Other Poems. New York: Random House, 1935.

Such Counsels You Gave To Me and Other Poems. New York: Random House, 1937.

The Selected Poetry of Robinson Jeffers. New York: Random House, 1938.

Be Angry at the Sun. New York: Random House, 1941.

Medea. New York: Random House, 1946.

The Double Axe and Other Poems. New York: Random House, 1948.

Hungerfield and Other Poems. New York: Random House, 1954.

The Beginning and the End and Other Poems. New York: Random House, 1963.

Robinson Jeffers: Selected Poems. New York: Vintage, 1965.

The Selected Letters of Robinson Jeffers., 1887-1962. Edited by Ann Ridgeway. Baltimore: Johns Hopkins Press, 1968.

CRITICAL ESSAYS

Poetry, Gongorism and a Thousand Years. Los Angeles: Ward Richie, 1949. Reprinted from New York *Times,* January 18, 1948, section VI, p. 16.

Themes in my Poems. San Francisco: Book Club of California, 1956.

SECONDARY SOURCES

BIBLIOGRAPHY

Alberts, Sidney. *A Bibliography of the Works of Robinson Jeffers.* New York: Random House, 1933.

Nolte, William. *The Merrill Checklist of Robinson Jeffers.* Columbus: Charles Merrill, 1970.

Vardamis, Alex A. *The Critical Reputation of Robinson Jeffers.* Hamden, Connecticut: Archon Books, 1972.

White, William. "Robinson Jeffers: A Checklist: 1959-65." *Serif,* 3 (June 1966) , 36-39.

Woodbridge, Hensley. "A Bibliographical Note on Robinson Jeffers." *American Book Collector,* 10 (September 1959) , 15-18.

BIOGRAPHY

Adamic, Louis. *Robinson Jeffers: A Portrait.* Seattle: University of Washington Bookstore, 1926.

Bennett, Melba. *Robinson Jeffers and the Sea.* San Francisco: Grabhorn, 1936.

———. *The Stone Mason of Tor House.* Los Angeles: Ward Richie, 1966.

Greenan, Edith. *Of Una Jeffers.* Los Angeles: Ward Richie, 1939.

Sterling, George. *Robinson Jeffers: The Man and the Artist.* New York: Boni and Liveright, 1926.

CRITICAL STUDIES

Brophy, Robert J. "The Apocalyptic Dimension of Jeffers' Narratives." *Robinson Jeffers Newsletter,* No. 32 (July 1972) , 4-7.

———. "Landscape as Genesis and Analogue in Jeffers' Narratives." *Robinson Jeffers Newsletter,* No. 29 (August 1971) , 11-16.

———. *Robinson Jeffers: Myth, Ritual, and Symbol in His Narrative Poems.* Cleveland: Case Western Reserve University Press, 1973.

48

―――. " 'Tamar,' 'The Cenci,' and Incest." *American Literature,* 42 (May 1970) , 241-44.

Carpenter, Frederic I. "Death Comes for Robinson Jeffers." *University Review,* 7 (December 1940) , 97-105.

―――. *Robinson Jeffers.* New York: Twayne, 1962.

―――. "The Values of Robinson Jeffers." *American Literature,* 11 (January 1940) , 353-66.

Coffin, Arthur B. *Robinson Jeffers: Poet of Inhumanism.* Madison: University of Wisconsin, 1971.

Everson, William. "Archetype West" in *Regional Perspectives.* Chicago: American Library Association, 1973. Pp. 207-306.

―――. "Introduction" to *Cawdor Medea* by Robinson Jeffers. Cayucos, California: Cayucos Press, 1971. Pp. vi-xxx.

―――. Introduction to *Californians* by Robinson Jeffers. Cayucos Press, 1971. Pp. vii-xxxvi.

―――. Introduction to *The Alpine Christ and Other Poems* by Robinson Jeffers. Cayucos Press, 1973.

―――. Introduction to *Brides of the South Wind* by Robinson Jeffers. Cayucos Press, 1975.

Flewelling, R. T. "Tragedy: Greece To California." *Personalist,* 20 (Summer 1949) , 229-45.

Gregory, Horace. "Poet Without critics: A Note on Robinson Jeffers" in *New World Writing* (April 1955) , 40-52.

Gilbert, Rudolph. *Shine, Perishing Republic: Robinson Jeffers and the Tragic Sense in Modern Poetry.* Boston: Bruce Humphries, 1936.

Hotchkiss, William. *Robinson Jeffers: The Sivaistic Vision.* Auburn, California: Blue Oak Press, 1975.

Lutyens, David. "Robinson Jeffers" in *The Creative Encounter.* London: Seeker and Warburg, 1960.

Miller, Benjamin. "The Demands of the Religious Consciousness." *Review of Religion,* 4 (May 1940) , 401-15.

Monjian, Mercedes. *Robinson Jeffers: A Study in Inhumanism.* Pittsburgh: University of Pittsburgh Press, 1958.

Nolte, William. *The Merrill Guide to Robinson Jeffers.* Columbus: Charles Merrill, 1970.

―――. "Robinson Jeffers as Didactic Poet." *Virginia Quarterly Review,* 42 (Spring 1966) , 257-72.

Powell, Lawrence C. *Robinson Jeffers: The Man and His Work*. Pasadena: San Pasqual Press, 1940 (1934 edition updated).

Rexroth, Kenneth. "In Defense of Robinson Jeffers." *Saturday Review of Literature*, August 10, 1957, p. 30.

Squires, Radcliffe. *The Loyalties of Robinson Jeffers*. Ann Arbor: University of Michigan Press, 1956.

Waggoner, Hyatt H. "Robinson Jeffers" in *The Heel of Elohim: Science and Values in Modern Poetry*. Norman: University of Oklahoma Press, 1950. Pp. 105-32.

Watts, Harold. "Multivalence in Robinson Jeffers." *College English*, 3 (November 1941), 109-20.

Wilder, Amos N. "The Nihilism of Robinson Jeffers" in *Spiritual Aspects of the New Poetry*. New York: Harper, 1940. Pp. 141-52.

Winters, Yvor. "Robinson Jeffers." *Poetry*, 35 (February 1930), 279-86.

For an exhaustive annotated bibliography of books, articles, and reviews on Jeffers from 1912 to 1970, the reader is referred to the invaluable *Critical Reputation of Robinson Jeffers* by Alex A. Vardamis, cited above.

The Robinson Jeffers Newsletter, a quarterly sponsored by Occidental College (1962 to date), publishes News and Notes of Jeffers events, Publication Notes, Queries, Reviews, Abstracts, Research in Progress, Short Articles, Explications, Memoirs, and an ongoing series on Jeffers Research Materials.